Thoughts from the Heart:

Embracing Change and Finding Love

Copyright © 2025 by Christine Palmisano

All rights reserved.

ISBN 978-1-62806-461-2 (print | paperback)

Library of Congress Control Number 2025913282

Published by Salt Water Media
29 Broad Street, Suite 104
Berlin, MD 21811
www.saltwatermedia.com

Cover image and interior images are courtesy of the author

Thoughts From the Heart: Embracing Change and Finding Love

Christine Palmisano

I dedicate this book to my mother, who always talked about being a writer and inspired me to take words and grammar seriously.

To my husband Mike, who believes in the nearly impossible, makes it happen, and made me believe that my words were worth sharing with others.

To Opa, my beloved father-in-law, who urged me to publish my first book but passed away before I could get it into print.

To the writers and artists I have read and met along the way, thank you for inspiring me by your work and honesty which moved me in so many ways.

Author's Note

As a child I would write or tell stories and not worry about what people thought because they were for me, or my audience of one or two. When I "grew up" and had a job where I wrote for others in a style that they reviewed, rewrote, and then approved, I forgot that I had my own style and I stopped writing on my own time. Now, in the final chapters of life, I remembered that I love to write for me and my audience, whether one or one hundred. This anthology of poems written over the past few years is my first foray into opening my heart and exposing my writing to others again. I hope you will find some value in it, to include sharing in my reflection and emotional journey, and maybe we will build a connection along the way.

Contents

Prologue i

Chapter 1: Family Ties 1

    My Mother 2

    Mom 3

    My Dad 4

    The Empty Chair 6

    Bittersweet Goodbye 7

    My North Star 9

    Sweet Sixteen 10

    Unmet Expectations 11

    A Son Like No Other 12

    Mike 14

    Annie 15

    Pure of Heart 16

    Opa 17

Chapter 2: Heart Prints 19

    Jimmy 20

    Mayor of Velocity 21

    Loss of Kane 23

    Bright Light 24

Chapter 3: Life Transitions 25

    New Day 26

    Sunny Day 27

    Sound of the Sea 28

    Heartbreak 29

    New Beginnings 30

    Return as a Rooster 31

    Waiting for the Music 32

    The Unmasking 33

    Cobwebs 34

    Dazed and Confused 35

Chapter 4: Starting a New Chapter 37

    Another Year 38

    Chill 39

    Holiday 40

    Last Day of the Year 41

    Stuff 42

    Lost in a Sea of Doubt 43

Chapter 5: Spiritual Reflections 45

    Seeing the Unseen 46

    Wine and Shine 47

    New Day Two 48

    Daybreak 49

    Deep Wounds 50

    Waves 51

    The Soul of My Tree 52

    Today is not Yesterday 53

    Snowcaps 55

    Sanibel Shells 56

    The Ace in the Deck 58

    Bittersweet Moments 60

    Denali 62

    Turning the Page 63

    Day of Sorrow 64

    What's in a Name? 65

    Loss of Control 67

    Reflection 69

    Faded Memories 70

About the Author 71

Prologue

When I started writing poetry in 2020, I was exploring what to do in retirement after 35 years of working and leading others in the intelligence community. I was used to a long daily commute, managing in a secure and often predictable bureaucracy, and had grown comfortable with my "work family" after decades of interaction. My personal life had gone through a lot of upheaval after my divorce in 2013. I resisted and then leapt into a new, longterm relationship with Mike, whose personality could not be more opposite that that of my first husband. I spent many hours worrying and losing sleep as I tried to build an adult relationship with my son who was angry, sad, and struggling to deal with the changes in our family, and was on his own bumpy journey in life.

As I pulled together the poems written from late 2020 to 2024, I was amazed at how much changed in a few years. The worldwide pandemic altered our family interactions and decisions about health, politics, and each other. Our favorite vacation spot on Sanibel Island was destroyed by a hurricane of historical proportions, which prompted conversations with Mike about whether Florida would remain our home As an international relations major and avid traveler, I often viewed myself more as an observer of world events than a participant. I have learned so much by authentically sharing and exposing my heart, and strongly encourage all of my readers to do the same.

Chapter 1

Family Ties

While they say you cannot pick your family (blood relatives), it is also true that families either stay close or drift apart depending on how much effort is expended to remain and participate in each other's busy lives. I have been blessed to have a caring albeit somewhat dysfunctional birth family as well as an amazing, and often equally lively, extended family joined through marriage. This series of poems honors some of the colorful members of my family and may remind you of someone in your family.

My Mother

My Mother
There is no other
Who collects knick knacks galore
Always claiming no more
Pictures on the walls everywhere
Reminding her of those not there
Keeping the family together
Via many texts through the ether
Always ready to give advice
Thinking she is being nice
Worrying all the time
Not aware of the sublime
Eager to please
Her enduring love will not cease

January 3, 2023. "My Mother" reflects her love of collecting items she displays around the house as well as her passion for family pictures and posting them everywhere. A typical doting mother, she seems eager to help her children regardless of how old they are, and is ready to offer advice with the best of intentions.

Mom

She is an unusual one
She lives to be in the sun
Giving her inner child flight
She loves to celebrate her birthday with a fright
Ghosts, skeletons, and ogres abound
Too much Halloween cannot be found
Sharing the experience is best
Shrek and most decorations in jest
Her real spirit lies in family
Not satisfied to let them be
She calls, texts, and shares galore
Always striving for more
For in this link
Is her true happiness I think
We cherish her silly ways
These make for memorable days
There is no other
Like our wonderful mother

October 20, 2023. Another homage to my mom, this one is lighter than the last but still highlights her quirkiness that makes her uniquely our mother. With her birthday in late October, she fully embraces Halloween and has celebrated it in different and sometimes goofy ways over the years, including throwing parties with the house decorated (including a fake, bloody body in the tub), and going to Fright Fest in Orlando (at 80 years old).

My Dad

Growing up you loved to play sports
Football, wrestling, and all sorts
You taught me to be strong
How to stand up for myself, and still get along
You encouraged me to fly
To keep reaching for the sky
With every new vacation we took
I gained an experience not found in a book
I yearned for more
To see many a shore
So once I grew
Off I flew
I didn't come back often enough
Each time I did, you'd share some new stuff
Stories about sacrifice and service
Struggles that made you nervous
Cracks in the armor began to appear
Drawing the family near
Fixing your heart
Led to a new start
You have repeatedly shown death the door
Fighting back for more
Your indefatigable spirit has taught me the most
So on this Father's Day, it is you I toast
I am so glad
To call you my Dad

June 20, 2024. Not to be left out, this reflection covers decades of lessons and life with my dad. Covering his life from his childhood, through my teen years, and now through one medical emergency after another, our family has been amazed by how often he has beat the odds to live another day.

The Empty Chair

Grandpa used to sit there
In that big, brown chair
He would sit and stare
Looking out there
I would wonder what he thought
Wondered for naught
Grandpa didn't say a lot
He just sat in that spot
His repose
From what only he knows
Now the chair is bare
I wish Grandpa was still sitting there

May 28, 2021. Written about my grandfather, Frank Janezick, who was born in March 1908, married my grandmother in 1934, and passed away in December 1981. He loved trains. We would walk along the train track together and he would share stories about his earlier life and the days when the trains still passed through the neighborhood. Otherwise, Grandpa didn't say much to this young girl who was starting to become quite independent as she grew up in a 1970s world of women's liberation and expression.

Bittersweet Goodbye

As my plane touched the ground
I returned to a home once again found
I came from quite far
Filled with memories driving the car
My focus is on the grand dame
My 99-year-old grand mam
Her roots were simple but strong
Which is why she lasted so long
Now it's time to let her go
Not much left to show
Her thoughts no longer clear
Her words hard to hear
While it's difficult not to weep
I know it's her time to sleep
Prepare for the journey above
Lifted by all of our love

April 16, 2021. Written about my grandmother, Emily Filtz, who was the matriarch of a family of nine children and stayed in a small cabin after she sold the larger house in northern Wisconsin. Living alone after my grandfather passed, she had a bad fall and developed dementia. She was under the loving care of my Aunt Linda and others before she passed about a week after my visit. She was

tough but she also enjoyed being goofy at times. I remember her boisterous laugh and how she loved Tweety Bird. She was often found cooking when the large Filtz family gathered. I remember scaling freshly caught fish with her one time—that was messy! In her limited spare time, she loved to go bowling.

My North Star

Some women stand out from the crowd
She stands regal and proud
Her sense of fashion I envy
Her wit can match me
Her wisdom I often seek
For she is not meek
She is a sage
Who gets better with age
So dear "aunt" Patti
May this birthday be
The best one yet
As we plan for another set
You are a blessing in my life
Let's put behind this pandemic strife
It's time to plan our next date
Then your birthday we will celebrate!!!

April 30, 2021. "Aunt" Patti appeared in my life after I married my first husband. While our divorce ended our marriage, it did not end this very special relationship with Patti. We learned how to dance around the difficulties of no longer being "family" but still remain united in spirit and friendship. There are few people that I can count on more than Aunt Patti who shares out of love her unvarnished truth and tells me what I need to hear, not what I want to hear. Through her love and guidance, I have made better decisions and become a better person. A cancer survivor several times, she also has been a great example of celebrating life and so generous in helping me do that as well.

Sweet Sixteen

A day like no other
A shift from one stage to another
Full of Life's possibilities
This day reflects on these
For the beautiful, bright, young woman you are
Is now apparent near and far
Enjoy this day
In your own special way
Sending much love across the miles
Hoping this day, week, and year are filled with many smiles

April 28, 2021. Written in honor of my youngest niece, Peyton, as she turned 16. It is always hard for me to hit a family milestone and not to be able to participate in the celebration. This was my way of showing how much I cared on this special day.

Unmet Expectations

I stand alone at the sink
Nothing but time to think
Wishing my son was here
Not upstairs but more near
Distant in his computer game
Trying to build his team's fame
For our vision is not the same
My ideas he labels lame
I pray he finds his way
A passion he follows some day
For in these four walls
I know his dream stalls
Out there somewhere
Is the future I swear
Pray Lord that he can see
What his talent and hard work in the future can be

April 6, 2021. Written about my son who was struggling to find work and meaning in the midst of the COVID pandemic. Already in his 20s, he and his friends were influenced more by social media than I was during this period. I continued to hope and believe in future opportunities while his network became more cynical and dystopian. Learning how to raise my son was not easy given innate differences in communication. I tried to direct less and support more (sometimes with "tough love") as I strived to build our relationship along the way.

A Son Like No Other

When I became a mother
I tried not to smother
I may have directed and led
Setting expectations from sunrise to bed
I learned too late
Not everything needed to be done by a certain date
For my son was like no other
What he needed most was his mother
Someone to cheer and listen
Someone who would notice what made his eyes glisten
For what made him stand out
Was not the things I thought about
He could cite ancient battles and destroy virtual beasts
His Guild was not interested in the least
In the grades he scored
Or what made him bored
They wanted to know what skills he brought
Was he better than the other lot
Alliance or Horde
Exploring new worlds seldom made him bored
For he's a new generation
One the history books will mention
For these new age sons
Have a different way of learning, and getting things done
Stretching through work and still having fun
He has become someone friends depend on
He is a great man
Kind, reflective, and often quick to take a stand
He may feel anachronistic

But the values we share, I'm glad they did stick
He is a son like no other
I'm proud to be his mother

December 31, 2023. Written more than two years after "Unmet Expectations," this was inspired by an end of year reflection. My son had a new job, had moved into his own place, and was paying his bills. Our relationship was improving and maturing as we both appreciated the more limited time we had together throughout the year.

Mike

Mike is the man for me
Despite how many differences there may be
He is always ready for adventure
Saying things out loud that I try to censure
But his love for me cannot be beat
In the middle we work hard to meet
Because our love for each other is strong
Time apart seems too long
Our days are unpredictable
Our love of family invincible
When we reflect on the days past
We remark, what a blast!
The path ahead is unwritten
Together the pieces are knitten

July 21, 2024. This poem reflects my relationship with my husband Mike, including our unpredictable, zigzagging path of discovery. Every day we learn more about how our upbringing, experiences, and personalities influence how we think and how we blend our families over time. We have shared great joy in our journey as we travel widely, navigate time with our complex families, and prioritize how we want to spend these later years together.

Annie

Annie is the mother of four
But she is so much more
She can run a marathon without even trying
Most of us would be dying
She has a gift for finding the joy
Within each and every boy
She makes you feel welcome
Even on the days when it might not be fun
I don't know how she keeps it together
During COVID there was so much to weather
I am blessed to be part of her clan
I look forward to spending time together whenever we can

July 19, 2023. My daugher-in-law is truly a marvel with a huge heart. This poem honors many gifts she shares and the bright light that shines from within. Not having a daughter, I relish the time we spend together and wish we did not live so far apart.

Pure of Heart

How does one start
To describe another pure of heart
She always put others first
Helping them through the worst
Every stranger a potential friend
Thinking of others to the end
Gathering those around her she loved most
Reminding all in one last mass of the Holy Ghost
Her spirit lives on in those who remember
Especially those she bore in August, November, and December
Of her pound cake we did boast
And today we toast
A wife, mother, grandmother, aunt and sister we loved most
With her memory we carry on
Living life while she watches from beyond

February 19, 2022. On the anniversary of my sweet mother-in-law's passing, I honored Margaret Madden Van Zandt (a.k.a Peg or Peggy) in the only way I know how. She was so generous in spirit and selfless in ways I know I am not. She is greatly missed.

Opa

I'm the contrarian
He's the grammarian
Steeped in history
Always ready to teach me
About events long past
WWII memories long last
Revered for his medical care
We meet past patients everywhere
He sells his book night and day
Meeting so many people along the way
His rosy outlook, key to longevity
Leaving behind an amazing legacy
An advocate for staying strong
He walks and pushes his cart along
97 years young
His song will be sung
But not before he shares another story
About his many days of glory
Skiing with Howard Head, Bill the Kid, and famous skiers
galore
Traveling the world and so much more
But family songs and tales are the ones he loves the most
To each special member we raise a toast

January 4, 2025. I ended 2024 with the sad knowledge that my father-in-law, fondly called Opa, would not be around much longer due to a brain tumor that doctors found three days before Christmas. Mike and I were blessed to spend a lot of quality time with him in 2024. I was pleased that he liked the poem after he read it. Opa did add a comma. :) He passed away on January 24, 2025.

Chapter 2

Heart Prints

As we evolve as adults, we encounter people whom we meet briefly, follow others through social media, or see someone repeatedly over time who changes us. For one reason or another, these people make a deep impression, whether good or bad or often both, that leaves an indelible imprint on our heart. We may "know" them for a few hours, a few days, months or many years but it is something the person says, does, or shares that stays with us, and helps us to reflect and grow as a person. This series of poems honors some of the people who have left their imprint on my heart and made me a better person.

Jimmy

Today Jimmy Buffet died
I cried, and cried, and cried
He brought us Island music
And made me feel alive
We will carry on his legacy as we dance
And Sing
It's a Parrothead Thing!

September 2, 2023. Written in honor of Jimmy Buffet. A self-proclaimed Parrothead and a short-time member of the Parrothead club, his music is my go-to for times when I need to relax or revel in the joy of living. Seeing Buffet and the Coral Reefer Band live was a day long, big party. For me, a Jimmy Buffet concert offered a great time out with my friends and family and created lasting memories such as the time I introduced my sister to his music when we saw the band together in 2022. I know seeing Jimmy Buffet and the Coral Reefer Band over the past decade helped me take myself a little less seriously, and dance a lot more!

Mayor of Velocity

Mayor of Velocity
His smile we often did see
A quick stop to say "Hi!"
Or lingering to stop by
Many conversations we had
Sharing stories of being a dad
Or sports days gone by
He had an artistic eye
And introduced new friends
That legacy won't end
Let's raise our glass
To our mayor who has passed
Too young and too soon
A reminder for everyone in the room
Take a moment to count the blessings
Make good decisions on important things
His jovial greeting is missed
By too many to list

September 21, 2021. Written in honor of Kevin "Verb" Lamont Gittings who was 52 when he died. I met Kevin at our favorite Velocity Wings restaurant where he was a regular patron. He never failed to greet my husband and me with a smile and would chat, even if briefly, before socializing with many others. Kevin held many records as an athlete who played football, rugby, wrestled, and ran track. He was a self-taught engineer and enjoyed photography. Talking about family, he was quick to share how proud he was of his two daughters. His effervescent personality brought together regulars at Velocity Wings so I wasn't surprised when some of them began to drift away after the Mayor of Velocity departed.

Loss of Kane

This week we lost Kane
His passing hurts more than I can explain
While I never met him
Every day I tuned in to listen
His stories of Sophie and Sam were the best
I enjoyed when he put Intern John to the test
The morning crew is not the same
I'm not saying it is lame
It's just there's a hole where Kane once was
I listened every morning because
The group was like my dysfunctional family
Now I cherish the time listening to Kane in my memory

March 8, 2021. Written in honor of Peter Dribbler, better known to listeners as Kane. He was 43 years old when he died. As the poem explains, he was part of my typically more than one hour commute to work in the morning, and helped me start my day with a laugh as well as sparked reflection on the topic of the day.

Bright Light

You were born a bright light
To shine like a star in the night
Sharing tales was your joy
Inspiring others, more than a boy
Your time was not long enough
Especially for a history buff
You solved your own mystery
Hence your father you did see
Your chapter may be closed
But all those impacted, no one knows
Your light from above
Still shines on all you love

———

December 2021. Although I did not meet Sam Anthony, who was a special assistant to the Archivist of the United States at the National Archives, his wife Sharon told me loving stories about his professional achievements and his struggle with cancer. An extraordinary man who was adopted after being given up by his mother, he had the courage to find his father shortly before he died. That heart wrenching and lovely story was captured by the *New York Times* in "52 Years in 11 Days: A Son, Facing Death, Finds His Father," published on October 9, 2021. I encourage you to read the article and reflect on how amazing it is that a life well lived can touch others they never meet.

Chapter 3

Life Transitions

When I started writing poetry in 2020, I could not have predicted all of the transitions ahead, including the pandemic, a new marriage, moving to a new state following retirement, and my son building roots in a different city. This series of poems reflects the range of emotions experienced during rapid change from 2021 to 2024, including my uncertainty about my path ahead, some fears, some hopes and a bunch of optimism that things would somehow work out. I think it is that faith that keeps me grounded during tumultuous change and that faith has deepened as I have aged and returned to church on a weekly basis. My retirement poem is universally understood, but some of the other poems reflect one way to approach the world. I choose hope and optimism.

New Day

It's a new day
I wake up in a new way
A smile in my heart
Ready for a new start
Yesterday is gone
To prior worries, so long
I cannot redo the past
Forgive and forget must last
Look ahead
Time to create new memories instead

November 23, 2020. In the early stages of the pandemic, I struggled often to find joy and practice gratitude. This poem was a reminder of how every day was a new opportunity to make positive memories despite the negative media environment and constant reminders around me of people's heart-wrenching challenges as they too navigated uncertainty and a rapidly changing world.

Sunny Day

Oh, sunny day
Make my troubles go away
Mend my heart
While we are apart
The day may not be near
When we are together here
But you are on my mind
I'm sure that is shared in kind
Until we are together then
While we question when
Let's bring back the sunny day
After we chase those clouds away

November 25, 2020. Six months into the COVID pandemic, my then fiancé and I were trying to confirm whether our December wedding would happen. The situation changed weekly as the church and reception venue monitored conditions and local regulations. I was wistful missing my family and sad that most of them chose not to attend the wedding because of increased health risks related to traveling and being in a large group.

Sound of the Sea

Sound of the Sea
Not too far from me
Sun is rising
Each new day surprising
Who knows what lies ahead
I know not in my head
Rather it is what will emerge
Then forward it will surge
A new day
Bright in its own way
Maybe this day with a cure
For what ails here
For in my heart
I am ready for a new start
The sound of the sea does soothe
Time to rise and move

December 6, 2020. Lying safe in bed in our timeshare on Sanibel, I was reflecting on the beautiful sunrise, the calmness of the sea and its effect on me. I relished in the promise of each

new day. After six months of the pandemic, many people were hoping a vaccine or some sort of solution to "return the world to normal" was around the corner.

Heartbreak

When will I know
Whether it is a Go
Two guests less
What a mess
This disease has taken its toll
The Impact we do not fully know
How many will be left
Trying not to feel bereft
Preparing to walk down the aisle
And planning to put on one big smile

December 6, 2020. Just six days before my wedding in Captiva, FL, we were still receiving last minute cancellations from family members and friends. Our final count was 18, including Mike and me. As long as the church was performing the service and the reception venue was open, we decided to move forward with the ceremony. At this time, there was no vaccination and the risks of COVID were high for anyone with serious underlying health issues. In our discussions, many of those invited made their decision not to attend based on fear of the unknown. It was noteworthy to me that we ended up with more known Republicans than Democrats in attendance. No one reported contracting COVID from attending our wedding, which was held mostly outdoors.

New Beginnings

New beginnings are not about wins
Or losses
Or changing bosses
It's pushing the button Restart
Rejuvenating the heart
Finding the way
To begin each day
With a smile
That lasts for a while
Let's toast to a fresh start
And opening each and every heart

January 1, 2021. Nine months into the pandemic I was working full-time while many employees were coming back to work after staying home. There were a lot of adjustments, and some resentments on both sides of the aisle. I also made a lateral job shift after "firing" my boss who frankly wasn't too happy with me either at that point. My new "boss" was more willing to be a partner, tapping my strengths and supporting some of my ideas to improve the overall organization. This poem was as much about trying to find things to smile about during some of the hardest months of the pandemic while also finding new terra firma after being on shaky ground at work.

Return as a Rooster

I want to be a Key West rooster when I come back
No one will give me flack
For they wander the streets all day
Going their own way
The King of all birds here
No one seems to go near
For in Key West
The rooster is ruler of the nest

January 10, 2021. My husband and I have had the pleasure and privilege to spend part of each January in Key West, FL. We love the live music and art culture and the generally great weather. We walk everywhere and typically encounter roosters roaming throughout the city where they are protected by law. This poem was inspired on a day that roosters were at my feet while eating breakfast on a patio at "Two Friends." I watched the roosters  meander across the street near Duval, and encountered them outside the post office where I was mailing a package. These bright, seemingly confident birds are an obvious reminder that you are in Key West!

Waiting for the Music

When will the music return
Missing the songs that burn
Into my soul
COVID has taken its toll
My favorite band
Is playing virtually throughout the land
Not quite the same
What they miss is not the fame
It's the cheer of the crowd
Shouting out loud
Some time not too far away
The bands will play
Bring back that day!!!

April 6, 2021. A shameless Bon Jovi fan, this poem was inspired after watching Jon Bon Jovi online as he tried to engage fans in penning some lines for a new song. After two decades of filling stadiums and singing anthemic songs, I imagined he felt the pang of missing the stage as well. I sure missed being part of that audience! What I had observed but didn't fully appreciate was that Jon was also going through his own struggle due to an atrophying  vocal cord. I have learned to appreciate every performance by my favorite singers as we are all in an age group where performances of the band's music is often being replaced by cover bands.

The Unmasking

For more than a year
We have lived in fear
Fear of the bug that we could not see
Fear of having company
But now most have selected
To get protected
The hour is here
When we can drop that fear
Take off the mask
Bring out the flask
It's time to Celebrate
Doesn't it feel great!!

May 14, 2021. While the pandemic would not officially be declared over for another year, this was the first point where we started to feel some relief following the delivery of the first COVID shots. Buoyed by the belief that they would be safer, people started to resume normal activities. We had so much more to learn about how we managed this pandemic—good and bad—after a year of government and self-imposed restrictions.

Cobwebs

Cobwebs block my view
As I struggle to find something new
Time to take off the blinder
Looking within to find her
For somewhere along the way
I lost that fierce, confident play
Now is the time to rise from the ash
No time to old views rehash
For the future is filled with possibility
Time to craft what that time will mean for me

May 15, 2021. Written as I started seriously preparing for retirement, I struggled with fear of the unknown as well as reflected on how much I changed over 35 years. Along the way, I had a few revelations. I recognized I had become too serious and lost some of my former spontaneity and craved tapping my creativity. I was seeking answers as I was hopeful but not sure about what I wanted to do next.

Dazed and Confused

Years of Labor and Devotion
Months of paperwork and preparation
A few hours of celebration and adulation
Then no sensation
Dumbfounded that it is the past
How long will this feeling last
It's time to turn the page and start a new chapter
Fill the days with laughter
For these have been often dark and busy years
Filled with long hours and many global fears
Yearning for the sun
Time to have some fun
Putting on bright clothes
Next steps, who knows!

July 30, 2022. Written on my last day of employment, this poem was inspired by the intense tumble of emotions that appears to be universal following the end of a long career. My heart was filled with hope but also doubt about the real value and meaning of the past 35+ years now that the events and career milestones were in the rearview mirror.

Chapter 4

Starting a New Chapter

Starting a new year and a new life chapter after working for more than 35 years in the same occupation and after selling my home of 20 years, I was excited by endless possibilities ahead. I also was unsettled as I tried and stumbled in paving a new path. With more time on my hands, I realized some of my goals remained the same, unachieved ones, and some had yet to be clarified. As I slowed down, I also took time to genuinely appreciate the world around me and to breath more slowly and deeply.

Another Year

Another year is here
A time to overcome what we fear
Often resuscitated goals of the past
New plans we pray will last
We pledge to do our best
To reach that lofty goal
To sail our ship beyond another shoal
For here we sit with optimism and hope
Not focusing on how we might again be the dope
For this year is a new one
Let's get going and get it done!

January 3, 2023. With New Year's resolutions in mind, the poem reflects on how many times we try, and try again, to set goals—often the same ones—and strive to reach them each year.

Chill

A chill is in the air
Leaves are everywhere
Crimson, burnt orange, and saffron
Explosion of color painted on
Gray, heavy clouds dim the light
Adding to the Halloween fright
Morning cold and warm lover
Keep me snuggling under cover
Pulling out the warm clothes
How soon and long a winter, no one knows
Hot cider, pumpkin coffee, and warm tea
Fall drinks delight me
Radiant orange Hunter's moon
Signals family gatherings coming soon
I prefer warmer weather
But cherish this time of year together

November 3, 2023. There is so much in fall that inspires me to celebrate the signs of the changing season. I especially enjoy the anticipation of my favorite holidays around the corner.

Holiday

Today begins the holiday break
So many things to make
The pies are baking in the oven
The oyster stuffing made for a loved one
Turkey defrosting
Is not the only thing
Green beans, yams, and potatoes too
A feast for more than a few
Now to pour the wine
As we prepare to dine
The meal will go too fast
The special exchanges will not last
Before you know it, that time is here.
Time to clean up until next year

December 18, 2023. We actually missed Thanksgiving in 2023 because we were on a Panama Canal cruise. Feeling nostalgic and wistful, I reflected on what made past Thanksgiving feasts special for me.

Last Day of the Year

Last day of the year
What do I hear
No Santa's cheer
No Ho, Ho, Ho
Nor Christmas tree and mistletoe
For this year was really strange
So much travel and change
We moved hundreds of miles away
Only to realize we did not want to stay
For home truly is where the heart lives
And for our family, Maryland it is
So pack those boxes and more
Soon we will return to the Shore

December 31, 2023. When we moved to Florida, we felt cut off from family, including the grandkids, and friends who were still "up north." We constantly talked about whether to be "snowbirds" or "heatbirds," as Mike put it. We finally decided to move forward with a long delayed plan to bring us back to Mike's home state for the summer. Being "up north" also provided a reprieve from scorching Florida heat during those months.

Stuff

I have too much stuff
I once thought it was not enough
I bought things for so many reasons
Some to match the seasons
Pieces attached to a memory
I thought each piece was a part of me
But now my stuff is hidden away
Waiting to be sorted some day
Each item takes up space
No longer does my stuff have a place
Lots to give away
Saving that for another day

February 5, 2023. During the process of "cleaning out" and selling my house in December 2022, I realized how much I didn't need and how much would not fit with the new Florida and beach decor. Many boxes of household goods, books, personal papers, and and some furniture were "temporarily" stored. I planned to sort through it to donate, toss, or save a select few items—probably to be stored in a closet—but that took a couple years as well. When asked by a junior colleague what lesson I wanted to share, I told him to stop buying and holding "stuff" as soon as he could.

Lost in a Sea of Doubt

Lost in a sea of doubt
Wondering which way is out
Searching for the nearest shore
Looking for a door
Ah, to wiggle toes in the sand
Where will I land
For drifting at sea
Is no longer for me
Hoping to land ashore
To be filled with doubt no more

———

June 9, 2023. Nearly a year after I retired, we were traveling a lot due to my husband's work commitments, to attend family events in different states, and to go on vacation. I was certainly feeling adrift after living in one home for 20 years and now seldom being home. While I relished not having to get up for work anymore, and enjoyed exploring new vacation spots, our travel slowed establishing new roots and making new friends. I also was restless and looking for a new, heart-fulfilling purpose to guide how I spent my time.

Chapter 5

Spiritual Reflections

In this chapter, I share my spiritual awakening as I reconnect with my core beliefs and values through reflection, and spending more time in nature. Whether you believe in God or a greater force that binds us together, these poems are about finding that connection that makes us human; about reminding ourselves that love is more powerful than hate; and about how living in the moment is better than living in the past or obsessing about the future.

Seeing the Unseen

Not focused on the surrounding strife
We focus on building our vision of life
Outside our doors lie misery, and struggle we may not see
What is our responsibility to wake up and believe?
Do we open the doors and let the homeless man in
Or do we continue to push for each personal win
We have so many riches
Yet others lack loaves and adequate dishes
Perhaps it's time to set a new plate
Or has the divide made it too late
I pray for a new conversation
An open door for transformation
For all who claim to love Jesus
This is what he prayed for us

February 21, 2021. I try to remember the message of love and giving to others as I set my priorities each day. I have been bestowed with some amazing gifts and have the privilege of being born in a country of opportunity that rewards hard work. I pray that everyone can learn to approach life with gratitude, and take time to help the fellow "man" in need.

Wine and Shine

Tunes playing in the distance
Vines filling the vista
People coming and going
Wine still flowing
Feeling the warm glow
From the Merlot I know
Rest and reflection
This is the right direction
Not many hours left to burn
Until waiting for sun's return

May 15, 2021. After a day of relaxing at my favorite winery, I reflected on the pleasurable release of sitting back and enjoying a few precious hours with friends. Always so busy, we enjoyed the fruit of the vine, and being uplifted by one another as we shared stories and observed the signs of spring.

New Day Two

It's a new day
Get going in a new way
Yelling and shouting behind us
Fading memory of the fuss
Beginning with a loving heart
Committing to a new start
Trying again
To make it a win

July 5, 2021. I was overwhelmed at this point by the stress of being a year away from retirement, trying to figure out where my son would move after I sold the house, and finding agreement on long-term direction with my new husband. I don't know what argument sparked this poem, but it reflects the realization and reminder that each day offers a new start—a "do over" if you will.

Daybreak

Daybreak comes too soon
Light flooding the room
Where did night flee?
Why are you no longer embracing me?
Fading memories of a dream
Only moments ago, important did it seem
Thoughts of the chores ahead
Wishing I could stay in bed
Rise sleeping beauty
Time to start the day's work and fulfill my duty

July 14, 2021. Many mornings I lie in bed wishing for more time to rest and rejuvenate before facing a new day that I imagined would most likely be filled with familiar patterns. At this point, I may have been feeling more rebellious as I started thinking about ending years of conditioning and developed some delight in imagining that my morning routine would change after retirement.

Deep Wounds

Some emotional wounds cut so deep
Their pain continues to seep
Time will heal most
Until turned into a memory ghost
The memories of 9/11 are like that
I wear them like an old hat
One I don't put on much anymore
But on the anniversary they restore
Glimpses of a day long past
Lifelong changes that last
We lost many that day and since
Twenty years and new tragedies make me wince
May those who grieve like thine
Find healing grace over time

August 29, 2021. As we approached the 20th anniversary of the 9/11 tragedies in New York, Washington, D.C. and Pennsylvania, I vividly recalled the events and my experience working with terrorism analysts, while my sister-in-law picked up my son from school. This was the first year I could write with less pain and more objectivity gained from time. I was incredulous that two decades had passed. Many countries were still fighting terrorism and, in my view, the world had not changed much. I prayed for healing for those impacted on 9/11, as well as for those suffering losses due to the long-term impact of toxic exposure when the towers fell.

Waves

Waves lapping at the shore
Revealing shells galore
Boats in the distance seen
Bouncing on water gleam
Hunting for that perfect shell
Finding it, time will tell
City towers far away
There they can stay
Sand pipers scurry by
Searching for little fry
Pelicans diving deep
Fish aplenty they seek
Thunderous waves rolling in
Bringing sea treasures with them
Sea grass rising from the sand
Spread across the land
Altogether I see
God's beauty and the relaxing place I want to be

December 8, 2021. Written on Sanibel, these were among my favorite vacation memories. I breathed more deeply, loved gathering shells from the beach, and felt the joy of slowing down long enough to truly appreciate the beauty before me. I didn't realize how truly, painfully cherished these memories would be a year later when Hurricane Ian destroyed this part of Sanibel.

The Soul of My Tree

Standing tall looking at me
My weathered and aged oak tree
I see on bended knee
The gnarled and twisted limbs of my favorite tree
20 years have passed
Some didn't think the little tree would last
Tall and proud
My tree now shouts out loud
I'm still standing here
Weathered many a storm without fear
I'm a mighty oak
That's no joke

September 6, 2022. The oak tree was planted when we built our house. At some point, a section in the middle had split away, perhaps from a lightning strike, and my husband thought the tree might not survive. He advocated cutting it down. I insisted on giving the tree more time to see if it would adapt and live. Twenty years later, when I prepared to sell the home following my retirement, I compared how the mighty oak tree and I had survived two decades with some noteworthy scars but also continued to demonstrate a lot of resilience.

Today is Not Yesterday

Today I have cycled the sun 58 times
It took awhile to rediscover my rhymes
I was so busy working and growing
I didn't stop long enough to see how much I was knowing
I took a long pause for a year
Discovered some new things I fear
Time is slipping into the future so fast
I want special moments with friends and family to last
I listen more as they share their day
For in that is their special way
My body and mind are still strong
I don't know for how long
Some parts have broken and been fixed
Their rebound has been mixed
The things I used to lust
After a good try can be a bust
But appreciation for who I am and what I have is so much more
I know it's not the stuff but what is through each new door
So today I do my best
To keep on doing right because that's the real test
I know that Life is meant for the living
And meaning is found in the giving
Time, family, and memories I cherish most
I think more deeply about meaning and the Holy Ghost
Today I count each blessing
Giving grace, and less stressing

August 5, 2023. A birthday reflection, this poem honors the distance traveled and the journey ahead while knowing my body is showing signs that aging will not be an easy process. At the same time, I'm so appreciative of how much I have been loved, and feel a spiritual drive to keep giving back to those in need. Little did I know how much my giving spirit would be tested in 2024 as family members confronted serious medical issues.

Snowcaps

Snowcaps as far as the eye can see
As I fly overhead they call out to me
Majestic and serene
God's majestic scene
Towns scattered here and there
Mountains tower everywhere
Then lost below a cloud or two
Soon is lost that spectacular view

March 11, 2023. Inspired by a flight from Orlando over the Shenandoah mountains and back to Washington, D.C. in late winter.

Sanibel Shells

Sanibel shells are everywhere
Sitting in vases here and there
Constant reminders of days gone by
So many great memories that make me cry
For our planned annual pilgrimage is no more
As we wait to hear what they can restore
Our beloved Chapel by the Sea
It beckons and waits for you and me
We dream of seeing the lighthouse and Gramma Dots
The fate of our stomping grounds we know not
What will be back
What will the island lack
Hurricane Ian may have spoken
But we know the island spirit cannot be broken
Randy, Wendy and Milissa will lead the way
As we create the script for this new play
Coming days we will seize
As we make new memories

October 8, 2022. We were heartbroken after Hurricane Ian destroyed our Sanibel timeshare, the location that brought Mike and I together, and our favorite vacation spot. Every year we would spend hours on the beach collecting shells, searching for the rarest one, the Junonia. Vases around the house are filled with the varied, beautiful shells we brought home and a constant reminder of those great vacations. Randy Wayne White, a local writer, is one of the most familiar names and the inspiration behind Doc Fords, a local restaurant. Randy's wife Wendy, a talented singer, and Milissa, a gifted local photographer, also survived the storm and were rebuilding their lives in Florida.

The Ace in the Deck

Life dealt me what I thought was a bad hand.
Every big move required me to be first, to find new strength, to take a stand.
But within that deck I had an ace
There was a Queen waiting to take her place
I just had to find the way without a map.
Sometimes mistakenly taking the same lap.
Along the way I found magic to help me.
People who would offer me a light to see the path I could not see.
I stumbled, fell, and picked myself up again, searching for Galilee.
One day, battered and bruised, I saw OZ
The city of gold was real, not a mirage
I started sprinting then crying because time was running out
I began to sing and shout
For I found what I didn't know I was looking for
Soon I assume my Throne when I walk through that shiny door
From here I can now see all of the land I crossed
I am no longer lost
Spread before me is a boisterous crowd
Shouting out loud
Mentors, jokers, lovers, haters, and some who came late to the party
But they all have been cheering for me!
What a glorious life I can only now see.

———

September 27, 2023. In the midst of a course by Tony Robbins and Dean Graziosi, I reflected back on many successes, the obstacles along the way, and how I had blossomed over the years. Having just celebrated another birthday, the sense of time remained on my mind. I truly appreciated more than ever that my accomplishments were the result of both those who supported me, and those who tested me, or posed obstacles that forced me to confront uncomfortable truths, and grow along the way.

Bittersweet Moments

A few days together
Our hearts, our love the tether
For it has been too long
So many days apart are gone
Life flickers by as we age
Slipping faster toward the last stage
For friends are dying
There is no denying
We grasp the here and now
And cling to each other somehow
To get through grief
To find joyous relief
Cherish the young ones exploring
They are the ones worth adoring
The future lies in them
We praise Him
For life is a circle that links us together
Each meeting, each greeting, unbounded love forever

July 14, 2023. This reflects a dilemma I faced following the sudden death of a coworker who retired about the same time that I did. We had worked together several times, including in my last job. A special person, she was committed to improving how employees were treated and the work culture in an organization often focused on executing its national security mission above all else. I had to choose between her funeral or a preplanned vacation with family, including the grandkids. I felt somewhat guilty that I could not pay my respects in person, but thought she would have understood the value I placed on not missing family time.

Denali

A wind whispers through the tree
A beautiful song to me
Coal-colored peaks, snow-capped mountains reach for the sky
Sometimes Denali shines in the distance, oh my!
Bumping over paved and gravel road
Bus carrying a tourist load
Winding through 60 million miles of preserve
Dahl sheep, caribou, bears, and moose in the reserve
Trees in the taiga rising to meet
Snow in the tundra under feet
Cluster of golden grizzlies here and there
Arctic squirrels everywhere
A caribou saunters across the road
Barely noticing the bus load
Finally a sighting of the golden bear
Lying with her cub over there
No moose appear
Missed them I fear
A great visit nonetheless
For awesome sights, we are blessed.

July 25, 2024. Denali Park was on my bucket list and it took us a long plane flight, a train ride, and a bus to see it. Expecting more animals roaming around, it was a little underwhelming as the animals were in the shade and far away as they were also trying to stay cool in the unexpected, nearly 90-degree weather.

Turning the Page

Lying in bed, the sun rises
Coming are fall and disguises
Forming together
Birds of a feather
Coolness in the air
A slight breeze in my hair
Where has the summer gone
Pool days now bygone
Time to turn the page
As Mother Nature again takes the stage

September 4, 2024. Although a very hot summer, I was still wistful as I watched the signs of summer's more carefree days fade with children starting school and many parents returning to work.

Day of Sorrow

Today is a day to remember
The 11th of September
We lost more than 2,900 that day
In such a horrible way
Many shed tears no more
But it doesn't mean we closed the door
Because the scars and wounds remain
The earth is blood stained
It seems fighting will not cease
Until the dark pain's release
But what do we gain
With the hate and sorrow that remain
It's time to turn the page
End the rage
For life is a precious gift
Our hearts we should lift
Put down the gun and pick up the plow
This killing and anger must end now
God teaches us to love our fellow man
Whether his name is Thomas, Mohammed, or Abraham

September 11, 2024. Working in national security on 9/11, it took many years for me not to fall to pieces in some way each anniversary. Twenty-three years later, it's easier to be reflective and hope for a different future for mankind, even knowing the nature of war and power is unlikely to change. It's up to each of us to make a difference in the circles around us and hope it makes a positive impact on the lives we do touch.

What's In A Name?

Given at birth
A name can shape the view of our worth
Anthony, Tony, or Antonio
Chosen one shapes who we know
Short or long
May be celebrated in a song
One name or two
Marks fame too
Common or rare
May make one stand out everywhere
Adopted by marriage
May affect one's carriage
Do others see you anew
Even those who have long known you
Or do they stick with your first name
Seeing you just the same
Do nicknames redefine
Or reflect what is already mine
What's in a name
They are not all the same

March 14, 2024. Identity is developed in so many ways, including through what we call ourselves and how others refer to us. I have gone through two major name changes following marriage, with my first name remaining the same. Even that name has varied with Chris more commonly used among my friends, and Christine used in my professional life. This poem was sparked by my reflection on how others think about me after a name change, and whether that has changed or influenced my core identity along the way.

Loss of Control

When there is a loss of control
No one knows where to go
Some lash out at those they love
Some pray to God above
Others run the other way
Not knowing what to say
The path of least resistance may seem fast
But the sparks and harm may last
Rising to a higher level is key
Understanding all answers do not end with me
Time to step back and take the long view
What is old, what is new
What can I do
For now is not the time to despair
Remember a greater power is still there
And solace comes in sharing and praying with thee
Nothing can be solved one, two, three
For some things will happen as they may
We must just take it day be day

December 22, 2024. Written on the plane as I dealt with serious eldercare issues in two separate states, I reflected on what I could do and what I needed to let go. I'm blessed to be part of a family with members who trust in a greater power to help us get through the difficult times. The best we can do is work together by playing to our strengths, and acknowledge each of us is going through our own complicated emotions while trying to retain some "normalcy" in our own lives. Through the pain of dealing with these issues, we have found joy in new blessings, such as spending more quality time together and growing closer.

Reflection

Sadness creeps in of days gone by
Why, oh why, must I cry
Expectations umet
Sun that did not set
Promise of new adventures
Create new fissures
Path less travelled
Or inevitable
I now know
Pain also exists on the other side of the door
So does finding more
More of me
Exposing more for others to see
Writing my own book
Some will comment as they look
For I'm no longer hiding
This ship I'm riding
To each new shore
Until there is no more

July 25, 2024. Written about the demise of my first marriage and about how life is filled with trials and triumphs, this poem ends with the joy I have found. It highlights the journey to find the courage within to break down internal barriers to writing and sharing more of myself with others.

Faded Memories

Faded memories flicker by
Caught in the mind's eye
Some are happy
Some are sad
Some are good
Some are bad
But the ones I cherish most
Are the ones of those I now toast
Times we laughed and cried
Special moments we shared what's inside
Vacations where we went somewhere
Sun on our skin, wind in our hair
Basking in the love and joy of times together
These are the moments I want to remember forever

February 11, 2024. Juxtaposed with "Reflection" this poem focuses more on the beauty of sharing life and vacation time with others, and how vulnerability enables us to truly share love and live a more fulfilled life. As I age, it becomes harder to recall with clarity the details of events over the past 60 years. Although time passing helps soften the pain of difficult memories, it also leaves me wanting more connection to the joyous memories. An old card or a picture might lead me to examine those good times, often sparking an emotional experience that makes me smile, cry, or maybe just relish in precious time together. Memories may be fleeting but I deeply appreciate the special moments shared with people with whom I connected along the way.

About the Author

CHRISTINE PALMISANO - This is Ms. Palmisano's first book of poetry. She was shaped by growing up Catholic in a traditional suburb in Wisconsin. Her values and patriotism were influenced by being raised in schools that followed the "Golden Rule" and started the day with the "Pledge of Allegiance." From a family with a history of military service, Ms. Palmisano lived and worked for more than 35 years as an intelligence analyst and senior executive in national security in Washington, D.C. She enjoys traveling and visiting historical sites and churches in cities around the world to learn more about the people and culture in each place. In addition to reading and spending time with family and friends, Ms. Palmisano and her husband in May 2025 finished their quest to complete a half-marathon in each of the 50 states.

www.ingramcontent.com/pod-product-compliance
Lightning Source LLC
Chambersburg PA
CBHW071238090426
42736CB00014B/3133